THE SPIRIT OF

YORKSHIRE

JOHN MORRISON

HALSGROVE

First published in Great Britain in 2007

British Library Cataloguing-in-Publication Data
A CIP record for this title is available from the British Library

ISBN 978 1 84114 658 4

HALSGROVE
Halsgrove House
Ryelands Farm Industrial Estate
Bagley Green, Wellington
Somerset TA21 9PZ
Tel: 01823 653777
Fax: 01823 216796
email: sales@halsgrove.com
website: www.halsgrove.com

Printed and bound by D'Auria Industrie Grafiche Spa, Italy

Introduction

If Yorkshire is hard to pin down, that's because there are many 'Yorkshires'. There's the Yorkshire of milltowns still reeling from the collapse of major industries, where the 'muck/brass proximity quotient' threatens to go off the scale. Then there's the new, thrusting, dynamic, forward-looking Yorkshire: all business plans and executive waterside apartments.

There's the Yorkshire of great houses, built by families of note to glorify themselves, with money made from sugar and the slave trade. There are the terraced streets of back-to-back houses where people still nip next door to borrow a cupful of balsamic vinegar.

Best of all – for photographers, at least – is the Yorkshire of moors and dales, where sunlight chases shadows across the fells and you can lose yourself in the landscape. There's cricket on the green, and a full house at Headingley. There's a village illuminated – briefly, but vividly – by a single shaft of light; springtime in the Dales, with the grass laid like green velour; a moonscape of a limestone pavement, the clints defined by snow. Sometimes the spirit is found in the broad panorama, sometimes in a small detail in the landscape; but always it's the quality of light that makes the difference.

Hag Dike Farm, in Coverdale, stranded for a few memorable hours on the shore of a misty ocean.

A flowery track from West Witton, down to the River Ure.

Past a traditional Dales barn to the waterfalls near Keld, Swaledale.

Opposite page:
Few fish farms can have a better backdrop than this – the limestone outcrop of Kilnsey Crag, in Wharfedale.

A heavy sky – and a pair of barns picked out by sunlight – near Burtersett in Wensleydale.

Opposite page:
The distinctive silhouette of Ingleborough is the backdrop to a misty morning.

Sunset over Swinsty Reservoir,
in the Washburn Valley –
Yorkshire's very own 'lake district'.

There's room to roam in Rosedale, once a centre of ironstone mining.

Snow transforms a limestone pavement above Conistone, in Wharfedale, into a monochrome moonscape.

Opposite page:
An increasingly-rare opportunity to get the sledge out, in Upper Wensleydale.

A light dusting of snow around the farms and field barns in Upper Wensleydale.

Opposite page:
In the midst of winter gloom, the clouds part – for just a few seconds – to illuminate the village of Askrigg.

The wall building competition on a sunny summer's day at Muker Show, Swaledale.

Opposite page:
Judging sheep at Muker Show.

Winskill Stones, near Settle, smack in the middle of limestone country.

Swaledale from Crackpot Hall; if there's a better view in the Yorkshire Dales then I've not seen it.

Another track which tempts you to explore,
near the Wensleydale village of Aysgarth.

Opposite page:
By the time it has reached West Tanfield,
the River Ure is broad and calm.

The first game of a new season:
village cricket at Crakehall, near Bedale.

Opposite page:
The Guildhall, reflected in the River Ouse at York.

Dyson's Clock on Lower Briggate,
a familiar landmark in Leeds.

Opposite page:
Whitby's harbour offers protection
from the ravages of the North Sea.

Further up the Yorkshire coast at Staithes,
a fisherman moors his boat.

Opposite page:
All aboard the steam train, at Goathland: one of the stations on the North Yorkshire Moors Railway.

Stormy skies form the
backdrop to
Whitby Marina.

A tribute to the gardeners' industry:
Cartwright Hall, in Bradford's Lister Park.

Few villages fit as
snugly into their surroundings
as Burnsall, in Wharfedale.

Opposite page:
Somewhere in the distance,
silhouetted against a pale
winter sky, is Castle Howard.

Dawn in Whitby, where the River Esk meets the sea.

Opposite page:
'Top and bottom' houses stacked up a hillside in Hebden Bridge.

A colourful corner of Arncliffe, one of the loveliest villages in the Yorkshire Dales.

Opposite page:
A classic shot of Upper Swaledale and the flank of Kisdon Hill.

Nidderdale in sunlight, with Gouthwaite Reservoir in the distance.

Opposite page:
A pleasing geometry: sheep pasture near Malham, divided up by limestone walls.

Winter trees on
Woodhouse Moor, Leeds,
etched starkly against the sky.

Piebald horse against
a patchwork of
walled fields, near Settle.

Fine Georgian façades line
cobbled Frenchgate, in Richmond.

Mist and cobbles recreate Haworth
as a set from a Hammer horror film.

The vernacular architecture of the
Yorkshire Dales – this is Arkengarthdale – seems a
perfect match for such austere surroundings.

Opposite page:
A colourful display greets visitors to this
cottage in the Wharfedale village of Burnsall.

Holy Trinity church, a quiet retreat on Micklegate, far from the tourist crowds in York.

Riverside apartments in Leeds lit up by the evening sun, and reflected in the River Aire.

Easing a narrowboat through the locks
on the Leeds-Liverpool Canal near Gargrave.

Opposite page:
Evening comes to Scarborough's South Bay.

SH33

Looking down into Rosedale.

A sight that would have been familiar to the Brontë sisters: autumn mist swirling around Haworth churchyard.

A shroud of mist envelops a farm in Birkdale... like a film still from *Wuthering Heights*.

Opposite page:
A delectable setting for Gibson Mill, near Hebden Bridge, with nothing to remind us that children as young as eight were once put to work here.

The city fathers of York should hang their heads in shame
for allowing a car park to be built around Clifford's Tower.

Opposite page:
Grey skies over Semerwater, the largest natural lake
in the Yorkshire Dales National Park.

The Norber Erratics, in Crummackdale,
are boulders of Silurian slate balanced on blocks of limestone –
a classic site of what geologists call an unconformity.

A modest cottage within sight
of Rievaulx Abbey, near Helmsley.

York's Lendal Bridge – and Tower – bathed in evening light and reflected in the River Ouse.

Opposite page: Knaresborough, built overlooking the gorge of the River Nidd, seen from the castle.

It's obviously hard work... being rowed
on the River Esk at Ruswarp.

Hardraw Force near Hawes:
England's highest single-drop waterfall.

If you've got to this point in this Swaledale walk,
the Farmer's Arms in Muker is just around the corner.

Opposite page:
Pantiled roofs frame the Laurel Inn,
Robin Hood's Bay.

THE LAUREL INN

The Old Coastguard's Cottage, Runswick Bay, with the most uninterrupted view in the village.

Elbow high, head still and
front foot down the wicket.
Another ball is dispatched to
the boundary at Headingley,
the home of Yorkshire cricket.

The last of Yorkshire: an early riser finds a ringside seat as dawn breaks over Hull and the Humber Estuary.